Mêmewars

Adeena Karasick

Talonbooks   Vancouver   1994

Published with the assistance of the Canada Council

Talonbooks
#201 - 1019 East Cordova
Vancouver, British Columbia
Canada V6A 1M8

Typeset in Palatino by Pièce de Résistance Ltée., and printed and bound in Canada by Hignell Printing Ltd.

First Printing: February 1994

ACKNOWLEDGMENTS: Earlier versions of "Feminine "Secreture" appeared as "Contextatic Sophistry" presented at Gesellschaft für Kanada Studien Conference, "Gender Differences and Institutions in Canada" in Grainau, & as "Sophistical Dismemberment" presented at the British Association for the Canadian Studies Conference, "Difference and Community: Canada and Europe," 1992 (Leeds). It was re-presented as a Lecture for Canadian Literature, at York University (Toronto), April, 1993, & as part of a Canadian Literature Field Exam, May, 1993. "Feminine "Secreture" was translated for performance as "A Canadian Feminist Poetics" for the Centre for Canadian Studies, Universidad de la Laguna (Tenerife, Spain) in December, 1993, & was later re-worked for the Institute of Commonwealth and American Studies and English Language Conference, "Commonwealth and American Women's Discourse," January, 1994 (Mysore, India). Selected portions were further re-formed as "The Empress Strikes Back," presented at the SNDT Women's University (Bombay) January, 1994. "Rigor Mo(r)ts: Death of Objectivity" was presented at the "Deadlines Conference" at SUNY (Buffalo) March, 1993. "N[or]th of Ar(c)ticulation" was first presented at the EGSA Colloquium, at York University, March, 1993; was reworked for the Workshop on Canadian Studies at the M. S. University of Baroda (Vadodara), January 1994; extended for performance at the University of Goa, January 1994; & is forthcoming in "The Foremost Investigations Anthology," Colorado, 1994. A previous version was published in A Poetics of Criticism (Buffalo, 1994). Earlier versions of "POETIX" were presented at the "Poetics Conference," SUNYAB, March, 1993, & appeared in Writing from the New Coast Anthology (December, 1993). Further selections of Mêmewars have appeared in SinOverTan, Cabaret Vert, The Poetry Project, Oblek, TXT & Poetic Briefs. THANKS TO: External Affairs and International Trade Canada, Much Music, Radio York, CIUT Radio, Cable 10 TV, CKY TV, Winnipeg TV, City TV, Co-Op Radio & the Knowledge Network. Also to Warren Tallman, bill bissett, Rabbi R. Cahana, Ken & Evan Karasick, Terry Goldie, Darren Wershler-Henry, Virus 23, Raymond Federman, Charles Bernstein, Shelley Spevakow & Kedrick James.

Canadian Cataloguing in Publication Data

Karasick, Adeena, 1965-
Mêmewars

Poems.
ISBN 0-88922-344-0

I. Title.
PS8571.A74M4 1993   C811'.54   C94-910007-2
PR9199.3.K37M4 1993

for Michael

Genres are not to be mixed.
I will not mix genres.
I repeat: genres are not to be mixed.
I will not mix them.

[Jacques Derrida]

FEMININE "SECRETURE
(OR S'ECRITURE OF THE NIGHT)

According to Derrida, there is a distinction between the Sophist and the Poet: "The Sophist manipulates empty signs and draws his effects from the contingencies of signifiers..." (*Margins of Philosophy* 248) while the Poet is concerned with the interplay of signifieds. Feminine "Secreture deconstructs these oppositions, inscribing itself into a process of "poetic sophistry."

Historically, Sophistry has been a manner of discourse based on exclusion, hierarchy, repression. A thinking practice which legitimizes retention, Truth and closure. Sophistical rhetoricians argue persuasively. They **answer**.

A poetic sophistry, or **feminine sophistry**, problematizes: because the sophic voice can no longer be read as a phallocentric proposition of a truth based discourse. Instead, it's grounded in **trust**. And trust is constructed **out of** trust (thrust between doubt 'n debt). It doesn't pulverize relations but creates possibilities. Opens the closed circuit of the sign.

Sophistry (as Philosophy) is "legal." It carries on a discourse of justification, demonstration. Feminine "Secreture however, is **lethal**. Does not justify and demonstrate — but in fluent effusion; enflamed she is a con(fusional relation which is "illegal," poetically dangerous, delegitimizing and upsetting.

Dislodging herself from the symbolic laws of rigid, logical discourse, colonizing rubrics of classical rationality, she works at once both synchronically, operating linearly along the paradigmatic axis — and diachronically — proliferating outward along the syntagmatic axis: her "form" challenges notions of meaning production. She's not incommunicable but communicates contemporaneously, interlinearly.
She's excessively reasonable.

So, within the curve of a question, her answers s(w)erve

frustrate, trouble and make strange)

But as signs occuring as a surplus supplement a centre, she's not **nonsense** but is **sensual**. A surplus of sens. Sensational, she's a profusion of sens. A consensus of since or **Sehnsucht** (desire)

She's not "non sense" but a nuisance — in nuance annoyance, pneumena gnomen ad nauseum: Anamnesic noematics or noetic acts

She's not rational or irrational but **relational**. An "improvisational logic" with **reason** vs **use**. For she does not **USE** but **DIFFUSES**.

Grounded in a struggle for power — and seeing that power is focused in the **control** of the metropolitan language — her tactics are not those of logical argumentation, but of disruption, subversion, transgression. Although she's writing against systematic thought, pragmatic logic, she's not **ILLOGICAL**. For illogical is what lacks logos, what is silence. Feminine "Secreture operates with an unanswerable logic, "flux logic" — where the consistence of truth has been lost. She's not silent, but explodes into a language infinitely resurgent.

And, just as she's not silent (only chains of differential relations) she is not absent but indistinguishable [as intermingling scents]. ((renascent)) She is absent like the desert: radically unmarked. "Absent" **not because it's not there** but because i can't **contain** it. Rhythmically immense, i can't hang on to it because it's twisting, shifting, folding **in on**. Similarly, she's in(excess)able.

So, Feminine "Secreture is not a writing of ABSENCE but degenerescence, dehiscence, **ABCESSES**

A con(fusional r(elation

WHERE "SHE'S A LITTLE BIT DANGEROUS"

operating as a **Femme Fatale**
where the fa (fathers) tale gets retold
as he comes and becomes

A fatality
because she's fatal — to die for

:a **dangerous** supplement
irresistable, resistent, insistant

She's a fatal distraction —

which shatters, staggers and overturns

to boldly go where no man has gone before

interrogating a Foucauldian "apparatus of colonial power,"
rewriting "the Royal road to colonial fantasy" (Bhabha),
"rethinking," she rethinks thinking itself — [where the ink thinks].

So, through a schizop(oetic)hrenic strategy, her writing becomes
as the Bhabaian fetish (predicated on mastery and pleasure **AND**
anxiety and defense). Subalternating, she provokes not through
tropes of mimicry, an appropriate imitation of academic (imperial
/ colonial) discourse, but through an excessive contextaticism,
Feminine **"Secreture** is a macrosyntactic signifying praxis that
both transgresses and respects the interdict. Designating and
distorting (as site and challenge) it's an instance of homage and
paracide).

De-colonizing the language, she seizes and replaces the discourse
of the centre, remoulds it to new usages — marking a se**para**tion.
It's an abrogative practice where she refuses the categories of the
imperial culture, its aestheic, its illusive standard of normative or
"correct" usage, and its assumption of a traditional and fixed
meaning.

Feminine "Secreture interrogates monist myths and foregrounds
the hybridized nature of writing. Installing the "interpretable"
within a familiar systematic framework, she abrogates the

privileged centralizing of "academic" discourse by using language to signify difference while employing "sameness." Maintaining distance and otherness while "**using**" the language she is continually writing within tension of centre and margin.

She writes as a pliant applies replies in a supple space — is spliced and splayed out **as content**. Where her form is not an extention but a textatic suspension. Where the content **is this**. Seated as strung moments abandoned as exeunt accesses.

— in excess of

As she edges into // a viral expanse // as these words throbbing through her groined in rough columns grated in a yawning of low arches strained violence slides / salvaged in residual remains / in distances as **certainty** swells / as accessories slap lashes torrents. sirens gust. as i repeat her liquid name that ripples softly in the corners

in **VIRTUAL SPACE**

An unterritorialized space — a passing product of words that's always shifting and unstable. which is always **[part-present and part-absent]** — always only **kinda there. Sorta there.** But **(SORTIE)** as a series of exits and entrances **is always uncertain**

So, Feminine "Secreture defies definition in a surplus of surfaces of continuous diminishing reference. in drifts and distances.

So, in the musk of fusing,
liaison sown
in **proximity** and **nearness**;

a pro**langue**ation — where her **(not-quite-there-yet)** is always **somewhere** — her **almost** coming, a continuous coming. As she comes and lets come. Keeps coming. Becoming not an autonomous, systemized whole, but systems of relations; systems of difference. **DEVIANCE** (as she links, develops and reproduces).

As she assembles, and reassembles in a moving ensemble, she writes not the **excluded middle.** Because irremedial, en medias, it's a mess. Amassing as she passes. From point to point. As she doubles and redoubles the simple. Reproducing it **as** repetition. **AS IF** repetition: a re(P[A]T[A])ition.

which is not imitative :
but deferred : it is what it is : repeated
as the trace replaces —

she's **a transpoetic rupture**
rehistoricized —

So, in the risk of repetition, she brings herself down
to language.   Routed **out of**
contextatic excess

Contaminated by memory /
confided and

exiled
Among her.

                              ...if the femme fits —

she starts / /
with F.M. frequency, **with** and **toward** beginning.

Celebrating not the lucid but the ludic. As the ludic colludes, she puts language **into** play. As she **comes out** and plays. Played out in a field of interplays. Ploys. Plies. Plais or placates with "**ways of gaming.**"

So, in the game and the gamble of the gambit, she runs the gamut of the gramé, as ellipsis eclipse in the lapsus. In the appearance of play, she **re-produces**
image and representation in a constant movement of simulation. Because the "outside" can not be reflected but is always already being produced. **VIRTUALLY. AS IF. ALMOST.** She's dispersed in currents fused in resonance.

It's never **OVER** but **OUVERT** as her oeuvre opens

(over and over into)

an opening of openness —

Never **CLOSES** but **CLOSE TO** —

she's

(A FEMME FOETAL)

which (as potential) **makes** possible
A pause sybility, which cannot be retained. Contained. Possesed. But comes and lets come. Caresses. as
a chorus of catechresis re-creases

Because she can't hang on to language, to meaning, she doesn't **hold on to** — but holds open — Feminine "Secreture is not about **HAVING** [To Have and to Hold] Because what she **HAS** is a [Not Having]. She **HAS** "a hunger **to give**" — She's got a **MOBILE HAVING**

As she gives herself up to and takes account of, 'cause she doesn't **HAVE** "the truth," "the meaning," 'cause language is always irreducibly metaphorical.

She never GETS IT

'Cause it's working by tropes and figures. Language is never literal. Is always something other.

So, Feminine "Secreture is foregroundly ambiguous. Undermining its own "meaning," it's always inscribed in differance, deferral —

[she used to be undecided, but now she's not so sure]

semestressed in understatement

she swallows, swells as sweat
spills
splits
apart, proliferates. Dis(emanates — staging, suspending and breaking loose.

excentric, spatial, mobile —

IT'S NOT ABOUT DEPTH

But explores surfaces. It's not reading for the SECRET. But the S'ecrit. The secret that SECRETES. S'ACRETES.

Feminine "Secreture is not mysterious writing; a **well kept** secret; but a secret that **dwells**. She conceals the secret which she shelters in her very readability.

Therefore, Feminine "Secreture is self reflexive. Speaks about this operation of surfaces of constructing and deconstructing borders. She's a b(order blur. or deborder excess. As aborders deborder folds
into her wry gypsum limbs
grinding myths meaning moistened in
her rhythmic shifts
as she sways into — and rubs against, presses up against, as she reaches for me as i wear her

in excess
in the axis of address /
as she stresses and cross-stresses / her full length gowns me in
skirted margins as /
mere meaning shifts —

as time
or in time, for this time

tempting
time becomes textual

Through an echoic ecrit, her contretemps intimidates what's past, present. For, when past is resonant. (sated in a series of strung moments) there's a profusion of presence.

a porous process of
appearance

as she swerves **away from**
when she is whet with, swells

in the longtemps
in the too langue lingering,

her round sori nodes in its rootstock.

AUTO[]GRAPHING

(what i ought to and ought not)

[graven]

graft. grifting (as the gift gives) forging or
forgetting / what forgoes or goes for —
(as so far grows)

because she's

A FAIME FATALE

famished.

inscribed **in** and **through** desire —
she's dire **[se dire]**
as she s(peaks herself into language
desired **by** language
languishes in or
langues for —

ME / ME = **Meme wars**. when i am a unit of knowledge
   virally replicating in language.

Meme (French = self same)
Meme (13th letter of the Hebrew alphabet. Signifies the middle)
Meme (as in Hebrew, mayim = Torah, water)
Meme (as in Hebrew, Makom = the name of the name naming
   this place of displacement which begins and ends with
   a Mem)
Meme (as in Greek, mneme = memory)
Meme (faulty mammary implants)

                     meme i me my maybe

as memoir mirrors pro-mises. mise-en / my memory as myriad
masks
invented **as** language. **in** language

re-membererd in indeterminate endurance as meme memes me in
mimesis **it's got to be [meme.]** when i am **[only a memes to an
end]** And **i can't sememe in myself because i am simulacric**. a
memetic mutation. (in the memetime)

eenie meenie miny moe.

me moi my myth
This moiety
cutting smaller by halves —

what i have and have not —
heaves / hovers
as meme means me:

   [maybe]

              mneme
              'n meme.

so-called or scalded
as a conch call courses,
caressed in
she calls forth

and though unruly, it's not a "liberating free play," a loss of limits
— an amorphous circulation of signification. Because it's **always
being articulated from somewhere**. From a historical-socio-
institutional-ethico-political position (in discourse). As intention,
it's never an arbitrary "free flowing" process but a continual
practice of framing. As she gathers and frames herself into frames
out of frames reframed in inferent aims — 'cause her frame lock
locuted in flux — as affixes affects a focus of facts inflected as **a
flex of frames.**

So, it's not **FREE** but **OPEN**.
An openness that can not be reflected, mimed or reproduced.
An irrepresentible position or proposition

dislocated in multiplicity.

MYTHISTORY

a palimpsestic historicity which is **HERESAY. HERSTORY. A
HERESY.** Retiled in a telling. A taling a toiling a taling seeing and
essaying suspecting and scandalously violating a perpetual
present.

So, though parataxing;

NE PAS DE HORS TAXE

She pays **duty**. A duty of responsibility.

She is not irresponsible, but
a response of depense
sybilance.
pennance.

*

Instead of looking toward the monolithic enterprise of the transcendental phallus [a transhistorical archetype leading to object identification]

an epithetic fallacy

where pen is penis) —

<u>IS</u>: signalling **PRESENCE. BEING.**

she reclaims **PEN(is)** where **PEN** suspends. depends. spends. impending. Appended. Upends. Where it not longer **PENS IN** but **O(PENS.**

(as panacea pends)

Not pen(**insular**)
but **p'ancillary**

She writes with penâche.

celebrating multiplicity, diversity. The body in flux, in process. Not inscribed in **LACK**, in **ABSENCE** but **SLACK**: **[EXCESS]**. Not **LOSS** but **LAWS**.

Because [what is lost in a loss of what can never be **possesed**] she does not **possess** but **processes**

So, in a process of veiling and unveiling. of folds that faintly flailing fall and fold in on. A sacred space that is both **secret** and **readable**.

Not the mystery, the black hole. not the SECRET but the S'ECRIT

S'ECRE(A)TURE OF THE NIGHT

For, when **DAY is Blinding. Present. Luminous. Transparent.**

she risks entry into
uncertainty —

surrenders

herself as
night thresholds her

as shadows, scars
spread out against —

dividing
her light
or sleight of [] as
simulacra come

[S]ECRITING

this body

(as the unconscious): an economy of production and culture — and therefore not a myth of ideological cohesion. A debasing stability

Not a differential product but a productivity of difference.

Because she's not writing from her "essential" female body: her for(bidden body. But, the forboding body — the body unbidden, between the body (**corps**) body (**text**) that bodies, embodies, bides into an ever expanding body.

So, when gender difference is located in an external and nonessential place between Female and Male, genetic code (as genre code) becomes a GENDEROUS ECONOMY. **A Paracidical ECONOMY where bodies feed off bodies to de-stabilize** the notion of sexual identity. — As identity, in terms of race, ethnicity, nationality, religion, class and age can no longer be seen as stable or even coherent

Gender MUST BE REVIEWED AS variable, provisional and constructed.

Feminine "Secreture is not a "Woman's Writing" — countersigned **by** Women **about** Woman **for** Women. But has to do with a textual-political practice.

The question is not: How to write **AS A WOMAN**. But how to write **AS IF A WOMAN**.

Because, she's a shifter. a diectic. Always already VIRTUAL.
BEYOND AND BESIDE.
Always already under erasure.
Not sublime. But subLIMINAL — Always on the edge of.

— As she edges into GENRES, GENDERS, GENII — FORGING THE GENIUS OF HER GENDER GENRE. SHE'S GENETICALLY RECOMBINANT

[TALKIN' 'BOUT MY GENDER N'ERRATION]

And her body is always already BEYOND and BESIDE her.

Her body has no place, but bodies **between**, bodes well, swells: this supple place spliced per space splayed out in hyperspacial interplays.

As her body streams in sign waves:
Sensorious, sinuous, sensing — she's not a **PLACE** but **PLAISIR**: **PLAYS** of
mounds and crevices where she **opens** herself from within herself. A presence that is no **WHERE** but is the writ(h)ing, the lips, the wound. Inscribed in diffusion, liquification. An unterritorialized space marked by crevices and pockets. But her pockets overflow. She pockets herself in a texture and folds into **a virtual space**. An (n)e(u)rotics of space. **Duration.**

Because her body is parts.
Always already a(part **of** and **apart from.**
The body bursting. body burning. Body
is not "**well defined**" but her definitions **s(well**. Surface between (the) body and () erasure of the body erupting. her frame surges; a surrender descends resounding in an insistent resistence.

She is marked by a multiplicity. Her body 'syncrisis. Is **battered, wounded, ruptured**. Is a translinguistic excess. Figuratively **dis-figured**. (go figure) Fragmented in bilabial syllables. Ellipse about her face, a farce, a fable. Effaced as her face lifts re-phrased in face value **FRAYS** as she faces up to and fascinates —

Because this body **IS A THINKING BODY**
Not subordinated to reason.
And not divorced **from it.**

An **ANTI-BODY** — which at once cleanses and defiles. Heals by making sick. Poisoning. Contaminating. **Tainting.** (When taint is excess) she excises
(Post-haste) Hosting foreign bodies. which she doesn't **absorb**.

But, between absorbtion and impermeability, permits entry into —

a patacidical sucking where her body corps body text is a synechdoche diectic where dis[sic]ecrit dis-eased in metalepsis. Abcesses. In
a sapirous reciprocity, where

The body proper poisoned is improper and inappropriately propelled into the

BODY CORPS BODY [ENCORE . ENCORPS]

A body of traces. as catechresis retraces appearance, and departs as sediments cling,
in a contaminated language.

Not the EROTIC BODY
but the ROTTING BODY
The WROUGHT BODY

written as a libidinal band — e(merging resurgent as
multiple subjectivities inscribed along shifting axes of influence.
A series of contact zones in a conflictual arena. A transferential
nexus or contextatic excess —

Where "the body-instrument opposition no longer holds." Affected in effect, this flex of affection infects **MAN** / **WOMAN** not as distinct and rival universes, but (as Self / Other Same / Different Presence / Absence Speaking / Writing Intelligible / Sensible)

it's a false duality.

Not a pair, but aperity. A partie. Parabolic,

A FAUX-PAS-DE-DEUX

A modular duality. En mode. Made. Modelled on. Destabilized, it's not that this dyad does not exist, but it's a difference without reference or reference with out (particular) Referent.

So, irreproducible or
Irreducible, **the deuce is wild.**

seducing, it's

"the super in**DUCE**ment of the superin**DUCE**ment," and
There is no absolute fronteir —

no inside / outside binary because what's outside is also intimate / so, it's not **A PAIR** but a paras/citical process. As sites excited (excided) re-s/cited as insite out, (undecided as apposite sites) reside in a site of desire

when plus is **more**
she's a parapluie.
a paradox

Both outside and inside because

that limit **is** always already transgre

Therefore, she can't work outside of the law. Because there is nothing outside of that law. She can **take that law — And smash that law apart.**
Work from within the law and exceed the law. She's not destroying the law, but **destorying.** Because it's a de**con**struction. A destruction that is always already another construction. As she cons and connaises, co(i)ns [in economies of exchange] / / as coincidence
consorts both in and out of canonical control —

[As vast as she can]

cons as

**the lacunian can
['cause she mixes it with love
and makes the wor(l)d / text good]**

So, she's not **seduced by** the symbolic order and then abandoned for asserting her presence within it, but **seduces** the symbolic order and abandons herself within it.

— Unsuited for —

pseuded or sedated: she's sated, asserting new walls, borders, screens, mirrors, laws. [f-laws] FABRICATED: fluid, effemeral, enflamed in
fluent effusion,

she flies away with language —

So, it's not a matter of **either / or** but **both / and. INCLUSIVE.** Destabilizing the notion of a National translatable language, she writes between linguistic cultures and codes, orthographies: generating a collaborative discourse that is simultaneouly private **AND** public.

In interlingual slysdexia **AS IF** translation, she medleys in a moving middle; a muddle. Infinitely devisable, translatable, mutateable. And her arguments are not "well structured" : because every structure has a centre and her centre surges.

So, decentered, she is (as a Bauderillardian city) infinitely extendible. Therefore her sophistical discourse is an erotics of space vs temporality. As she spaces herself out in new wor(l)ds, linking, ammassing, as she reproduces, expands, re-aligns, extends, she is **beyond and beside** the body and the body of her text.

where they're **LIKE** in their **DIFFERENCE**

**when you "like it like that" SIMULACRIC
when you "Take it like a [woman]" or
METAPHORICALLY — AS A WOMAN or
VIRTUALLY — AS IF A WOMAN**

She challenges notions of **SIMILARITY AND DIFFERENCE**

Because the SAME IS ALWAYS SOMETHING DIFFERENT

She challenges autonomy, stable identity; a capitalist vision of literary originality where ownership is a prime value. Questioning propriety by favouring an appropriative process of collage, assemblage, bricolage, parody, pastiche, quotation, she collectively shapes topoi, images, allusions, thieving, lying, cheating.

SHE BREAKS AND ENTERS — BEGS, BORROWS, STEALS

translating a literary tradition of consistency and cohesion into an **echonomy** of

EXCHANGES

> "if 'n given"
> this grift
> given to / or gifted by /

> in the grammar of the
> graft.

For, raising the stakes
what's at s(take
is taken as

> m(i)s{takes
st(r)oke

against all odds or
at odds

her auto-
graphics grind
in lockstep sweat

> slides

>> between her body text body corps
>> (en coeur) encore de la core
>> enc(h)or(e) accrues as
>> anacrusis corrodes

>> in desire.

In a spectral economy the spectator is part of the spectacle, the vision is never pure. I can't separate myself from these words merging because Lettristic clusters become directly synecdoch of the gaps, caesuras and silences which exist between the language which is the signifier of power and the experience it represents. As in a spectral economy the spectator is part of the spectacle, the vision is never pure. I can't separate myself from the total Lettristic clusters become directly synecdoch of the gaps, caesuras and silences which exist between the language which is the signifier of power and the experience it represents. As in a spectral economy the spectator is part of the spectacle, the vision is never pure. Lettristic clusters become directly synecdoch of the gaps, caesuras and silences which exist between the language which is the signifier of power and the experience it represents. As in a spectral economy the spectator is part of the spectacle, the vision is never pure. Lettristic clusters become directly synecdoch of the gaps, caesuras and silences which exist between the language which is the signifier of power and the experience it represents. As in a spectral economy the spectator is part of the spectacle, the vision is never pure. Lettristic clusters become directly synecdoch of the gaps, caesuras and silences which exist between the language which is the signifier of power and the experience it represents. As in a spectral economy the spectator is part of the spectacle, the vision is never pure. Lettristic clusters become directly synecdoch of the gaps, caesuras and silences which exist between the language which is the signifier of power and the experience it represents. As in a spectral economy the spectator is part of the spectacle, the vision is never pure. I can't separate myself from these words merging because just as in a spectral economy the spectator is part of the spectacle. The vision is never pure. I can't abstract my self from these words merging. I can't separate myself from these words merging because just as in a spectral economy the spectator is part of the spectacle. The vision is never pure. Lettristic clusters become directly synecdoch of the gaps, caesuras and silences which exist between the language which is the signifier of power and the experience it represents.

RIGOR MO(R)TS:
DEATH OF OBJECTIVITY

English Aesthetic Theory and Literary Criticism adopted the notion of Objectivity from Post-Kantian German theorists of the late 18th and early 19th C. The concept was soon naturalized and domesticated, primarily by Ruskin in 1856, and later by T.S. Eliot. Historically, Objectivity has been understood as a rhetorical strategy celebrating the definitive, detatched and the impersonal.

But if according to Lacan, only a Subject can understand a [M]eaning and every phenomenon of [M]eaning implies a [S]ubject, how can i separate Subject from Meaning. For, Meaning, as Object is a closed opening. An aporitic parody. Apperity. Appears in the folds of **exchange**. And therefore does not essentialize a differential product but a productivity of difference.

A Subject / Object binary must be restaged not in terms of a Lacanian mirror ["which establishes a relation between the organism and its reality [*Ecrits* 4] but a mirror that screens, shelters, conceals and shatters surfaces. Not **Lacanian** but **LACUNIAN**. **A myriad. A mire**. A mise en abymming beyond hermeneutic reflection. Beyond object totalization — where "the mirror / the error" as mirror murmers merge at the margin of méconnaissance. As i mis **take** you

If every time i look (re-garde) i contaminate, poison, make impure, the "you" can no longer exist as an entity separate from "me." As i cannibalize you. Ingested in a 'patacidical sucking — As a synechdoch deictic dis-eased in metalepsis. As ellipse slips abcesses in venemous reciprocity.

You can't **see me** — i'm a **semi**ological function. And what seems same assumes no "self-same" but solicits and separates in simile semes — So, even if i **seem** same it's only "effects" of the same. And you are not identical but eidedical; diectical, so you are **not the same or other** and therefore **disrupt the binary construct of illigitimate object vs legitimate subject.**

(And if "objectified facts may be regarded as variables" [Lacan]),
i form the object **out of** the object
as the object of this subject is an **act of construction**.

A constructive criticism because

Locating binaries is
an act of construction.
And, as a binary is a
metaphor and a ling-
uistic construct it
already exceeds itself
. is other. And if
each term is defined
by all the others it's
value is in relation
(so what's secondary
is not inferior but
triggers a reclaiming
which is always a re-
producing: Referencing
the hyper-referential
relations of dichoto-
mous discourse Locating
binaries is an act of
construction. And, as
a binary is a metaphor
and a linguistic
construct it already
exceeds itself. is
other. And if each term
is defined by all the
others it's value is
in relation (so what's
secondary is not
inferior but triggers
a reclaiming which is
always a re-producing:
Referencing the hyper-
referential relations
of dichotomous discourse
Locating binaries is
an act of construction.
And, as a binary is a
metaphor and a ling-
uistic construct it
already exceeds itself
. is other. And if
each term is defined
by all the others it's
value is in relation

(so what's secondary
is not inferior but
triggers a reclaiming
which is always a re-
producing: Referencing
the hyper-referential
relations of dichoto-
mous discourse Locating
binaries is an act of
construction. And, as
a binary is a metaphor
and a linguistic
construct it already
exceeds itself. is
other. And if each term
is defined by all the
others it's value is
in relation (so what's
secondary is not
inferior but triggers
a reclaiming which is
always a re-producing:
Referencing the hyper-
referential relations
of dichotomous discourse
(so what's secondary
is not inferior but
triggers a reclaiming
which is always a re-
producing: Referencing
the hyper-referential
relations of dichoto-
mous discourse Locating
binaries is an act of
construction. And, as
a binary is a metaphor
and a linguistic
construct it already
exceeds itself. is
other. And if each term
is defined by all the
others it's value is
in relation (so what's
secondary is not
inferior but triggers
a reclaiming which is

Therefore, the text cannot be "a historical object (a dialectical image) constructed in the materialist presentation of history separate from me."

["No we have no doubles / for we'd make a mess of duels / if we did" (Davies)]

So, as even the margins have margins — as a mirage merges a
Subject / Object distinction **is not binaric** but r(elational and
shifting. So, in the appearance of a double,

i'm a virtual complex.

Operating both synchronically **AND** diachronically, this opposition
collapses in an inseparable simultaneity. interpenetrating
the syntagmatic **AND** paridigmatic axes.

**A patadigmaxis
Patataxis in praxis
where subject meets object in**

An intersubjective oscillation
(O's elation) **between**
absorption and impermeability

In uprooted reciprocity,
not a pair but paroxysms.

[in repair]

i am dubbed in a redoubling

(and my doppelgänger is
a gang gone stranger)

Eingang

[A poetic convention].

So, i am not a movement from the Lacanian "specular" to the "social" i **am** social.

An inter n('err)ation. or an annotative n(ot)ation.
A dis[ema(nation) which **objects to** — a collective hysterical investment naturalized into a debasing stability — i'm multiple subjectivities aligned along shifting axes of influence. A series of "contact zones" (Bhaba) negotiated in a conflictual arena of eroticism. A paracidical process of supplementation, rupture and displacement which inform an interdiscursive and political practice.

So, i can't fetishize the Subject, because i'm a myth. My'th slips as i create i out of i. And to fetishize the Object is to fetishize the dead. And if according to Derrida, "this double [in] reality, indeed is death" (Derrida 206) the Object is in(excess)able. Always already **Like / As** kin. A second skin. Peeling the i out of i: the uncon**tain**able; the inarticulable. As the object intersects, it does not contain, but carries forward. This main **t'ain** (uncer**tain**) contaminated in a 'patacidical main tennance. As maintenant de(tained) per tain twined or quanti(tain)ted. Because the object is not outside of these sides but resides in a site of desire re-cited **beside**.

The object is **on the side of**. Beside itself. **Apside**. "stray verso" sites incite-out and untoward. Because there **is nothing outside of**. Ne pas de hors text. This vortext of possibilities and substitutions

Because the **SU**[b]**JE**[c]**T is** the story. The n'errative. A wandering error.

[TALKIN' 'BOUT MAGINARY NE'ERRATION]

Dispersed in an impress. or promise of. a palimpsestic abcess. As an ensouciant insistence assembles, disembles in a moving ensemble that resemblées. As i explode **into** myself. As i **become** you — Deixis in excess annexes
the syntax enacts in parataxis.

So, **"C'mon get real"**

i'm **not the subject** but **superject** [Whitehead] **not the object** but **objectile** [Blanchot]

Interjected — i can't separate my self from my self writing the already written because i am "always already writing in writing" [Cixous], so to try to cut the writer from writing is to cut text from context is to remain protected in specificity, solidity

The text cannot be "a historical object" (a dialectical image) constructed in the materialist presentation of history separate from me. I am these words. **[TO DIE FOR]** Fused in resonance. In nearness. Suffused in resurgent surfaces

Reflecting no reality,

De'thing-in-itself is **[unreal]** it's only reality producing. Producing only "effects of the real" [Barthes] Really, i relay relics' residue (which is hyperreal, serial).

Objectively, speaking no —— i can't separate myself from these words because just as in a spectral economy, the spectator is part of the spectacle. The vision is never pure. i can't abstract myself from the "totality." I'm an extpectant spectre: **aspects** of.

So, how can **i** tokenize the text as an independent variable? It's a veritable variety. In perpetual allusion, as the ludic deludes, it alludes to "nothing" operating only as a supplemental process of "Objective Correlatives."

"Chor-a"r(elations).

Distantiated **in desire**.

Decimated.

Because the object is **nothing in itself**. Is always supplemental.
Spliced and splayed in subtle play
Because "there have never been anything but supplements" [OG]
so i can't distinguish between what's essential and what's
accessory. [The Object is not an accident of the Subject but an
extension of an extension. A textatic suspension. As accesory
acceses in the nexus in the praxis of address

So, i'm not **"the perfected OBJECT"** or **"the subjective given"**
(which targets, splits off and decontextualizes) but gives over to /
gets taken as an inter(sub)jected abject. Objectivist echoes or
"object projections," as l'objet delies in irreducible slides.
elides. As i object to: question, conflict and contaminate.

Because the **object is artifice**

A hyperabsorptive orbit which
enfuses subjectivity **into it**

into "an indeterminate, extraintentional differential production
ejected between forces and intensities

Between desire between
u'n me when i name you anew

when the object **is this**.

L'OBJEU: between **the object and the object.** This passage of play
Appelez — as i **call into** / as
i come **out in** / **A field of interplays**
pulls / places / plais or placates.
ALMOST (AS IF) an object (objeu)

:an **objet trouvé.** (Found and said but not captured). An
"objectivist sensology." insensate sans or resonant sens / a
consensus of since. As i enter your senses. A conscientious
objector. A [con(sent(i)entious] ejector —
which **rejects** "l'objet-petit-a" (as **a** (autre) differentiates the other
from the Other.

but O / i say O / i will O — it's a

concentrated illusion of autonomy — As O others in another other —

(in or out[h]er)

when the same is always something other:

Dissident if i'd,
i'm other to my self or **a** self of others

as diffidend defers to

I O' U   **indebted**

or detonated

"when i feel so different"

"when you make **all the difference**"
as differ (nu)ances or the differing errances,

i'm just a system of difference

For(t) DeA(th) is **as** l'objet-petit-a. is **as** petit mort. because there is always already more and more **[morés]**. L'iAses. Reproduces. Multiplies. **[Fuckin' A]**
FRAYS Death **AS** the "supreme spAsm" (A's IF S(if)ting between homonomy / anonymy a liminal anomoly. A metamorph an amorphous morphology amour de la mort. a moratorium. post more t'aime.

RIGOR: to stiffen. rigid
(from hrigos) Rigid. Rigescent,
Rigorous (that which freezes)
Holds. Controls. Rigor (from Reg)
to move in a straight line. Direct.
Frigid. Frigus. Frigoris. FROZEN.
MORTIS: (from mer) to rub away,
damage. Dest(or)y [mors mort
mortem mo(r)ts melt]

de rigueur

And, if according to Jabés, the time of [death] is the time of borders crossed, orders deborder in deborder (excesses) align and live **on**. So, "textual death" is not as an experience of absence, lack, effacement, erasure, closure and silence but a series of traces and echoes inscribed in exile, rupture, movement and uncertainty.

["as death comes as a death to be died still more" (Blanchot)]

So, death can not be seen in terms of absence. Because there is no absence — Just a play of difference. Proximity. Duration. D'rifts and distances realizable or residable. Divisable.

Death is not **LOSS** but **LAWS**. Borders. Mirrors. Screens. Walls.

So, to objectify is to construct borders. But as boundaries blur, bond in an unbinding, objectivity is not theodicy by th' odyssey into an uncertain speculum

:a process of seeing and essaying suspecting and scandalously violating the "thing-in-itself."

Because i am always implicated.

So, as death enters me
(dwells in the open horizon of my measure)
how can i mourn for the fetishized object. When i slip between
presences, recesses.

i PASS AWAY

as depasser is to outdo

[en se passant de la mort]

i PASS[i]ON

[DEAD.
DIE.
WILL / DIE]

Because i cd not stop for Death

this end. **A DEAD END**. will end and end. Addended. Appended.
up ended. Dead ended. / Unending. Addenda ending.

You are dead now — And i am unavailable

(in the ordeal of ends abcess)

Because, if according to Lacan, the object needs a subject, and i am
an intersubjective abject **indebted** as dread's read
in / deed (as dit) speaks 'nded that ends on
this de(a)(p)th of surfaces,

THE DEATH OF OBJECTIVITY IS THE DEATH OF DEATH

For what's **DEAD** is not done. But is donne [(as gift) given with no giver]. As i am not **taken as** but **give over to** a thanotopraxis en proxy. in disintegration, vacant debilitation. Because it's not the **TERM** but **INTERMINABLE**. As i alliterate, obliterate in a cryptomorphic writhing. So, even if death is the "ultimate object," it's not the **perfected** object but **plusperfect**. A patatextual irriducibility that swells in an ongoing sacrifice out of sacrifice as i move toward the object measured by the object which **OPENS**. So, Objectivity is not a reductive, essentializing gesture of closure, as what's dead is never **OVER** but h'overs. **ouvert**. Opens **into** mounds and crevices: the corpus — bodies forth between the body (corps) body (text) for the beyond of the body is still the body: this libidinal band bound in the body and the body of my name.

So to name the unnamable, i name without naming: the object

Must Die.
Must Die.
The object O
the object O the object
Must die.

As death marches **into** a history of images: as a mirage merges where you always already are in excess (i'nexus of) borders blur boundaries overflow into all that is fluid en fluxus flooding **[As i read you ALIVE]** in the manner of a vortext. vertiginous vortices spiralling in striated surface s(tr)u(c)tures slain in virtual versions.

As an objective conjecture, conjunctive objector, because **Objectivity is always virtual.** — **AS IF** — As if the object was real. **As if it occupied place.** As residue constellates into the object which is always **as if** the object. — :a configuration of contours; sequences that wrenches security **out of** violent reciprocity exacerbated in objectivist checks. **"Because death is the extreme"** the extra meme. mismemed in a stream of memes

[semestressed]

So, i die and cannot die as death delivers in doubt, debt, detonated.

As i do without death

Because it *has* no dominion
and *shall* die, eidedic, paraphetic
Scarred *in* the valley of the shadow of [ ]

this dearth
driven or defyin'
the dyad dread dead.

NOTES

The object as "the mercury, the tain of this ink, forms a screen. It shelters and conceals. Holds in reserve and exposes to view. The screen: at once the visible projection surfaces for images, and that which prevents one from seeing the other side" This t'ain, this "stray verso." Inscribed, dismantled and denounced in an uncertain speculum.

This subject / object slippage may be read through the letter H or in Hebrew

 [Hayah] To be

Though this "signifies existence," "existence" always already requires connection with something else.

Therefore, subject is inextricably linked with predicate, producing object.

**[the existent that is the existent or
the arbitrarily necessary existent]**

Just like "the whole secret consists in the repetition in a predicate position of the secret in position, every word indicative of existence **or** "any system of writing exists **in itself** as the relation of an inside to itself,"

in desire,
The H is nothing in itself

which stages itself not as a Lacanian mirror (to recognize the "not-I") but as in bissett's, "mirror peopul" "whn we slide thru th glass slip so eezilee thru th layrs silkee n grateful merging n lyrikul blending into th reel intima n lusts uv th [] radians giving off th scent uv so manee n eternal mirrorings [] we fly thru...th sacrid corridora chanting n fanning our wayze thru...crystal caverna tremula...when the background becuming th foreground is whers th diffrens space is all space all space is all space...melt n curv into othr castuls medows othr consideraysyuns somnolent mirroring omni centring thru mor n mor mirrors we pass thru sheets in th splaying..." [*Inkorrect thots*].

Similarly, according to Derrida, "a mirror in not a source." Irreducible and pluspresent. It takes place — designed to be broken. "Since I am feigning not to know that my look can put even the planets turning in space to death, he who claims that I do not possess the faculty of memories will not be wrong. What remains to be done is to smash this mirror to smithereens" [*Dissemination*. Trans. with Intro. Barbara Johnson. London: U of Chicago P, 1981. 315].

Eingang: German: Object as a series of [entrances and exits]. But entrance, as opening, as a mirror is only a closed opening. An aporitic parody / aperity. Appears. As a distorting apparatus, it's a false exit. As the tain reflects imperfectly. Reflects images.

According to Derrida [*Diss.* 131] **Gift**, which means "present" in English, means "poison" or "married" in other Germanic languages.

Re: Doubling: According to Derrida, "we are faced then with mimicry imitating nothing; faced, so to speak, with a double that doubles no simple, a double that nothing anticipates, nothing at least that is not itself already a double. There is no simple reference" [*Diss.* 206].

A double without any first or last unity. Without death, birth or presence.

So, the object "remains both one and the other — both the [wo]man who manipulates words and the place where the unmanipulatable which language is, escapes every division and is pure indeterminacy" [Blanchot, Maurice. *The Space of Literature*. Trans. with Intro. by Ann Smock. London: U of Nebraska P, 1989.]

"Love can be the becoming which appropriates the other for itself by consuming it, introjecting it into itself, to the point where the other disappears." [Irigaray, Luce. *Elemental Passions*. Trans. by Joanne Collie and Judith Still. New York: Routledge, 1992.]

So, as in Deleuze's, *The Fold* [Trans. Tom Conley. Minneapolis: U of Minnesota P: 1993], [the object [] is manneristic, not essentializing: it becomes an event. As projection, unfolding, infolding; it assumes a place in a continuum by variation. No longer refers its condition to a spatial mold [] to a relation of form - matter, but to a temporal modulation that implies as much the beginnings continuous variation of matter as a continuous developement of form. Inseparable from a series of possible declensions or from a surface of variable curvature that it is itself describing]

Re: Death as abyss: not that which founds but the absence and the loss of all foundation. It does not have the solidity which would sustain such a relation. It is that which happens to no one, the uncertainty and the indecision of what never happens. [] It is its own imposter [Blanchot 154-55].

"Because death is the extreme," is
a possibility only, and to hide from it is to hide **in** it, i make my own death. I die and cannot die as death delivers in doubt and inauthenticity — starting from death...[s]he makes h[er] death; [s]he makes [her]self the power of a maker and gives to what [s]he makes its meaning and its truth. The decision to be without being is possibility itself; / the possibility of death [Blanchot 96].

N[or]th of Ar(c)ticulation

Within Canadian Literature, "The North" has repeatedly emerged as a dominating image of National Identity, and thus historically shaped the way Canada has been represented. However, through a sexist, imperialist discourse of mastery, idealization, and a mythology of cohesion, it has been framed as redemptive, ineffable, inscribed in silence, absence and purity.

As a multiplicity of voices, cultures, constructs, Canada cannot be theorized through an identity politics of purity. Therefore, it is crucial that "The North" be re-viewed not as a transcendent space of "mythological purification" (Smith, Scott, Campbell, Frye), not as the "candid virginity of the white [candida] page" but as can[a]da: Que NADA. KEINE DA — Not because there's "Nothing t(here) but because it's **kind of** — sort of. It never **is** what it **is** but is always **AS IF — ABOUT**. Not the "continuity of the nonscission" but a complicated materiality; a shifting presence of traces and echoes; inscribed in promise, image and memory.

Just as the sublime cannot be grounded as a philosophical (transcendental or metaphysical) principle, but a linguistic construct, "The North" must be re-viewed as a model of discourse; a tropological system.

Re-presenting the n[or]th through a language of rupture and displacement, foregrounds Canada not as a reified space that thematizes, essentializes and idealizes difference, but reframes it as differential system of networks and silences destabilized among shifting axes of influence. In the appearance of autonomy, it's not a differential product, but a productivity of differance. And therefore, the Canadian n[or]th interrogates a Eurocentric myth of Meaning; a regime of Truth, Authenticity and Representation; deconstructing an "apparatus of power" and the monocentrism of the colonial enterprise.

"The Canadian North performs nomadically"

As a hologramme which is not empty, vacuous but vascularly referential, the n[or]th resonates to radiate dis(emanate through a system that's simultaneously physical and oral, semantic sensory and metaphobic. As a hologrammatical moment, it must be theorized as a (n)e(u)rotics of space, duration, spectrum, range and latitude

where virtue becomes virtual becomes vertigo, legacy the league s'leurre salvation: sal(u)tation, where the pure touches on the impure and the empire (malempire).

Historically, the N[or]th has been marked by snow, and consequently theorized as ornament, accessory, precipitation. However, if precipitation gets recycled back into a system of sequential storage, snow then metonymically stands in for a supplemental process of relational differences; a complex productivity of pressures, masses and fronts.

Snow (as a crystalline stratum) forms by interiorizing and incorporating masses or amorphous material]. **Snowed in.** In s'nuance annoyance, inside moves outside so both outside and inside are inside ins/citing an out as sites reside in a s/cite of desire "inside out and untoward" — as "[t]he wintry silence [falls and] folds in" (Campbell) on a palimpsestic sustenance constituting multiplicitous concentrations, variations, intermediaries in a process of self replicating metastability. So then, if the metaphysical "is an empirical moment that necessarily remains external to the concept" [de Man], borders deborder in excess and the [meta] beyond is **as** when "the beyond of the n[or]th is still the n[or]th a syntactic surface thickly drifting in a network of **meta**-EUPHORICS

But snow, as "an economy of desires and discourses" [Godard], is fluid. Enflamed in fluent effusion, cannot be contained, enclosed. For [there'snow there, t(here] — it defies definition :diffuses in a surplus of surfaces of continually diminishing reference. Parergonic, "it disappears, buries itself, melts away at the moment it deploys its greatest energy" (Derrida).

So, as a heliotropic metaphor, which cannot be known in what is "proper" to it, snow conditions in the form of presence. Absents itself and therefore is the paradigm of the sensory AND of metaphor. In a polysemic twisting toward the n[or]th is a profusion of senses a consensus of since. As it slides eludes between difference (extensive sens)

Producing image and representation in a constant movement of simulation, energy, light. when the n[or]th is not reflected but always already being produced. Dispersed in currents, fused in resonance, in the appearance of **glas'** glaci-elated glare; glorified in a serial circulation that surrenders and says nothing.

Because the N[or]th is artifice. A hyperabsorptive orbit which infuses identity **into** it. Into an extraintentional differrential product ejected between desire. Between u'n me when i name u anew. When the N[or]th **IS THIS**. Not **absence** but abcesses through intersticial surfaces re-produced as

a profusion of differences, appearances that play in a locality (which is) an interlocuted linkage. — and as locus allocated in **likeness**, the n[or]th is a promise. a premise, palimpsesticized in an appropriative process.

[where the impress ha' snow closure]

where traces amass in a an'errative wandering **"whiteness"** "tu traces l'horizon" (Derrida) a horizontal network of differential echoes in exstasis where "the horizon melts" merges into the "horizon that held [her] together" merging scarless into "h'arisen" (bp Nichol) "her eyes on" (*Stone Angel*) an uncertain throbbing swelling through an inarticulate presence of d(rifts and di(stances performing in this aporitic play where disparity, aperity: a parody appears as aperture or portraiture where "border / lines are / border / plays" (Godard) played out in an intersticial s/cite.

So no, not referencing the pure and the chaste; the sober, restrained, firm and true, but as an ensouciant insistence assembles in a fugitive whiteness. Modulant and spectral, as i explode **into** the N**[or]**th, become the N**[or]**th

— Not i's 'lated —

but paratextatic

in a mechanics of fluids. en fluxus flooding. a "White Wall" upon which signifiance inscribes its signs and redundancies (Deleuze 166). But it's a "White Mythology." A suggestive whiteness in abundant light. Because "white can topple white into a fatal abyss of whiteness by claiming to be whiteness itself" (Jabés 181). "White's white shift / slips & / we drift on as the snow mounts" [Bk 6] in a hy[p]erarc(t)ic syntactivity of immanence in desire

Because the North is desire is that which i desire "as desire desires desire." In enigma and adjacency and therefore, is not the sign of hermeneutic purity, but [as "snow [that comes] **LIKE** a white present" (Geese 215) reflects, difracts — a(ban[d)onnes itself to synchronous currents in construct it never is what it is, as a "memory warp" that posesses neither meaning or trace, that which exists in its own disappearance. And i'm "clutching ravenously for a hold, something solid and substantial, something in which to reintegrate and repose — but it's [a]n effect of capturing a surface that becomes more enclosed the more it expands

So in the aporia of appearance, the N**[or]**th is dissimulated in a memetic drift, where meaning **becomes**. abstract surges entwined in an expanse of contours, as ice floes floods into "the sea [which] has no secret" as s'ecrit accrues in a twisting expanse. as an abacus cicada cascades ressembles around naked spectra eccentric. spatial. mobile — is enigmatic matter that melts **into** a memorializing memory an imminent amniosis which is **never pure.** As the forgotten begotten forgetting forgets. forges in a forgetful excess folds over in memorexile. **which is not meta but mimemata** en mimesis. Between synonomy / hononomy: a liminal anonymy. an anomie. a metonymic mimosa miming "the n[or]th" as a polyvalent multilingual activity which speaks to an ever changing historical moment.

And if "the time of the infinite is the time of borders crossed (Jabés 147), hologrammatological time is a process of b(ordering. A border blur which labours **about time.** An arctic time — not timeless but contemporaneous.

Not a frozen form (fermé) but performed as a forum or more for (a morph or)

For what was formerly far, is affirmed

Not as a s**NO**wscape but a s**NOW**scape. A moment that becomes "a history of images" that "faintly falling" flailing folds in on a palimpsestic historicity which is **HERE**say. A heresy. — So, it's not that the N[or]th as metonym has no primitive accumulation of time and therefore lives in a perpetual present, but having seen no slow, centuries-long accumulation of a principle of truth...lives in perpetual simulation, in a perpetual present of signs [Baudrillard]. Canada has "no neon history. No pioneers' blood bottled by a Coca Cola firm and sold as a 10 cent tradition" [Smart]. So, without revolution, there's no historical narrative easy to memorize. No Moment of Birth. Rather, a ritual of repetition, reproduced

as projection into —

"the northernmost north" [CS Lewis] an ar(c)ti(c)fact of N dimensions [Jabés]. **Ne pas de hors N[or]th.** When **Nth** (in)finite **OR** the possible posited in the probable; substitution. When **Nor th'** (is the negation of the p[ar(c)ticular) diffuses into the "North / quenched body" [Waldrop] n[or]th "of intention." [] of articulation. N[or]th mounting n[or]th / for when direction is a process of a compass [come to pass]; when context is essentially indexical, the n[or]th thrusting n[or]th is [not] th[is] n[or]th'is nor]th'at: (a whether pattern) Because **Magnetic N[or]th** has no stable direction — deflects in a relentless spectrum accumulative, cumulous. **AND** the **North Pole** is a pull. A play, appelez — as i call into the True North tru[nor]th which does not signify a mythological system of ideological cohesion, (but as **Due N[or]th, made** due: fort-da des dü) is always already a network of definition (as a veritable variety varies) virally replicating

So, the N[or]th is **not metaphysical but meteffusive.** always already metaphobic inscribed in image and translation. meta phasical. farcical. re-phrased in surpluspace... \ from sea to sea seized in hysteresis. ici. here now — So, just as silence is never singular [Jabés], the N[or]th can not be seen as a reified space but re(if)eyed. [to see and be scene] Possibilitized in a seeing and essaying suspecting and scandalously violating the N[or]th as a multiperspectival process

And, if Ar(c)ticulation means "the creation of an opening" then "c" the supplement ("From Sea to Sea" translated as "C - C") is seized as tropological specularity and thus Canada signifies a spectral economy of openings, ruptures, gaps

seethes in
caesuric seizures

So, without a fixed field of vision, the N[or]th moves from phenomenology to perhaps a "complex transphenomenality." An inevitable conviction of wor(l)ds existing within wor(l)ds. And therefore, N[or]th wards are all about sojourning. As the desert, they progress. Interlinearly absorbed in latitude, lunge into not **the end** but the **edge**. agon(e) abcesses in ice snow melt frozen skies in a void of terror. Always n[or]th becomes n[or]th dissolves in a drifting landscape and must be reviewed not as "a north thing called Nothing" [Nichol (*CT*)] but as "when not/hing comes unhinged" (Marlatt/Warland).

As the sublime (**as** the spatial ar(c)ticulation of the infinite) functions metaphorically defining itself in terms of extension —

When **i's so morphic**, the n[or]th (**as metamorph**) absorbing beauty, engulfs reason's resin **into** — an addictive diectic dislocated in wind clogged sonic waves of becoming the n[or]th **is** never the n[or]thing-in-itself but reckless and scattered as a collectivity inside an assemblage. For, when territorialization is an act of rhythm, t'errefied, it proceeds in a paratactic play

As a serial process where presence, place and time as excess **IS**

potentially metaphorical —**As if**— As if the N[or]th was s(if)ting through these letters. ad**rift**. as if i could posess the N[or]th **process** it as the N[or]th p(r)oses for the n[or]th (in)finitely substitutional. re-created in my{t[h([i]{s)tory}] which **as** the sublime **is** sublime because i construct it and make it sacred — (in a syntactic act) inexact and textatic — thres**held** by a twisting return toward the n[or]th as nation, a notion an annotative notation — a dis(ema**nation** that questions, conflicts and contaminates a mythology of cohesion in a struggle of silence as silence in disappearance where signs as values as revelation unveil

as polaraxis

or paralax/as the arctic tracks, contracts,

turns —

Circles at the edge of
ar(c)ticulation.

NOTES

The N[or]th cannot be theorized in terms of "the absolute," for if according to Deleuze and Guattari, "the absolute expresses nothing transcendent or undifferentiated, it does not even express a quantity that would exceed all given (relative) quantities. It expresses only a type of movement qualitatively different from relative movement. A movement is absolute when whatever its quantity and speed it relates 'a' body considered as multiple to a smooth space that it occupies in the manner of a vortex" then the N[or]th, inscribed in substitution, "opens a rhizomatic realm of possibility effecting the potentialization of the possible."

If according to bp Nichol, "S" is "the feminizer," then **Snow** is the feminization of temporality. [where the present drifts]

Snow as the Female Body (is not a fragmented, splintered body of organs — fragmented in relation to a unified body, but is a distribution of intensive principles of organs with a collectivity or multiplicity inside an assemblage.

Or, as explored by Deleuze and Guattari, snow must be reviewed as a crystalline stratum: where interior moves to exterior so both exterior and interior are interior; exteriorizing through replication, multiplication, outgrowths producing a multiplicity of perfect discontinuous states of metastability constituting so many hierarchical degrees (*1000 Plateaus* 50).

And, as in McCaffery's *North of Intention*, "North" is what always aready exceeds the text. In excess.

(Snow excess, or s'nexus)

Contemporary geograpoetic theorists have reclaimed the Desert as an image of "feminine ecriture." As the desert, the Canadain n[or]th is a [limitless perfect instantaneity of subjectivity, duration and "naked" space] : Nicole Brossard's *Mauve Desert*, by further extension, Baudrillard's *America*, Jane Rule's *Desert of the Heart* or Marlatt & Warland's *Double Negative*.

A Meme is an irrecoverable and slightly inaccurate self-replicating (id)entity with almost limitless power.

Memetics is concerned with **how** the message is translated

MEME   "a unit of cultural transmission or a unit of imitation"
MEME   (French): the same. La meme chose. choise. chosen
MEME   me replicating myself virally in language.
       Never alone: Me and Me
MEME = Me x 2 Me too. the same and other than

Mnemosyne: Memory [Greek]
Mneme: an unveiling (an un-forgetting)
Meme: (According to the Zohar: c. 13th C, Mem is the sign of passive action, creative power, and hieroglyphically signifies water. It is always used in the plural because Mem is collective, as water is the condensation of moisture.)
Meme: (According to the Bahir: c. 1176, "Just like the male cannot give birth, so the closed Mem cannot give birth. And just like the female has an opening with which to give birth, so can the open Mem give birth. The Mem is therefore open and closed.... What is meant by an opening? This is the direction of [N]orth."

WORKS (RE)CITED

Baudrillard, Jean. *Simulations.* Trans. Paul Patton and Philip Beitchman. New York: Semiotext(e),1983.
———. *America.* Trans. Chris Turner. New York: Verso, 1991.

Brossard, Nicole. *Picture Theory.* Trans. Barbara Godard. Montreal: Guernica, 1991.
———. *Mauve Desert.* Trans. Susanne de Lotbiniere-Harwood. Toronto: Coach House, 1990.

Canadian Poetry. Vol. 1. Ed. Jack David and Robert Lecker. Intro. by George Woodcock. Downsview, Ont.: ECW Press, 1982.

de Man, Paul. *Hermeneutics: Questions and Prospects.* Ed. Gary Shapiro and Alan Sica. Amherst: U of Massachusetts P, 1984.

Deleuze, Gilles and Felix Guattari. *A Thousand Plateaus.* Trans. and Foreward by Brian Massumi. Minneapolis: U of Minnesota P, 1988.

Derrida, Jacques. *Of Grammatology.* Trans. Gayatri Spivak. Baltimore: Johns Hopkins UP, 1976.
———. *Margins of Philosophy.* Trans. Alan Bass. Chicago: U of Chicago P, 1982.
———. *Disseminations.* Trans. with Intro. by Barbara Johnson. Chicago: U of Chicago P, 1981.

Dragomoshchenko, Arkadii. "Eroticism of For-Getting, Eroticism of Beyond Being." Trans. Vanessa Bittner with Michael Molnar. Presented at State University of New York at Buffalo, February, 1993.

Godard, Barbara. "Canadian? Literary? Theory?" *Open Letter.* 8th ser. No. 3. Spring, 1992.

Grove, Frederick Philip. "Snow."

Jabés, Edmond. *From the Book for the Book: An Edmond Jabés Reader.* Trans. Rosemarie Waldrop. Intro. by Richard Samelman. Hanover: Wesleyan UP, 1991.

Kant, Immanuel. *Critique of Judgement.* Trans. with Intro. by J. H. Bernard. London: Hafner, 1951.

Lacan, Jacques. *Ecrits: A Selection.* Trans. Alan Sheridan. New York: Norton, 1977.

Laurence, Margaret. *The Stone Angel.* Toronto: McClelland and Stewart, 1980.

Marlatt, Daphne, and Betsy Warland. *Double Negative.* Charlottetown: Gynergy, 1988.

McCaffery, Steve. *North of Intention: Critical Writings 1973 -1986.* Toronto: Nightwood, 1986.

Nichol, bp. *The Martyrology: Book 6 Books.* Toronto: Coach House, 1987.
———. *Continental Trance.* Lantzville: Oolichan, 1982.

Ostenso, Martha. *Wild Geese.* Toronto: McClelland and Steward, 1961.

Smart, Elizabeth. *By Grand Central Station I Sat Down and Wept.* London: Harper Collins, 1991.

'Because the facade is cut **into** :the surface suffused in locus recesses i am the image of my memory. Between synonomy / homonymy, ignonimy, anonymy: a liminal anomoly. An anomie. Am mimosa. A metamorph. An amourphous morphology. i'm a moment or second to myself. A historical image that **becomes**. A paracritactical passage. And as ellipsis eclipse in the lapsus — a repast of a past postulates as a resonant present sends espaced en an irrepressible present / as the wander of appearance expresences as possibility re-poised as pause / posit / post. se posed in a languerous re-pose.

So in a complex of codes i carry myself into a palimpsestic historicity which is heresay. A heresy. Retiled in a telling, a toiling, a taling. seeing and essaying suspecting and scandalously violating a perpetual present pre-sentiented in frictions. As fractions of fact infects fiction as a complex flex of conflictual flax for facts in flux is always infact fiction. So, retold there's a friction in the fiction as projection into as the fiction makes me re[e]l

"**C'mon get real**" i am a memorializing memory an imminent amniosis which is never pure. As forgetting begotten forgetting forgets. forges in a forgetful excess. folds over in memory murmers (as mere ages merge): a memorexile as i re-member to forget before memory and forgetting

in meme embers.

[As **re** created his name out of his **members**]

my history is an ideoleg[it(im)ization which i invent and reinvent as I demobilized shift into. A polyvalent multilingual activity which speaks to an ever changing historical moment.

I'm a "sign of the times"

(and take my time)

**[untime meme,
untie me]**

t'i me:

So, when **"it's all in the timing,"** it's ABOUT time —
tempered DOWN time (in a tropological time) — not
timeless, but **a temporal d(rift** — beyond and beside
time framed by the "no longer and not yet", by the "not
there yet and always already" of a tempestuous ges-
ture.

[i used to be a temporary sequitor]

when time is on my side, two timin' i tempt in no time,
'cause there's no time, when you know time — as this
text tears ON TIME as i bide time beating **this** time as
contaminated time —

taming, 'cause i am the image of my image: the
(n)e(u)rotic rotting. wrought. writ(h)ing the body
[corps] body [text]. For, when the **beyond** of the body is
still the body, i'm a synechdoc deictic where dis[sic]ecrit
dis-eased in metalepsis. degenerescence, dehiscences,
abcesses — displaced in an axiomatic excess: deixis in
excess annexes the syntax enacts in parataxis.

But with every look i **take from.** you. **steal away** in
images. Re-present you in an appropriative process. As
a premise a promise pro-mises **i am tied to you** pro-
pelled by impropriety. Palimpsesticized in erasure and
substitution. Because you are the miracle **of me.** And as
an instance solicits i steal **into** / elicit systems dissolut-
ed in elasticity lists — last lasts lost in list sills — **swells
into** a history of images: as a mirage merges where you
always already are in excess (i'nexus of) borders blur

boundaries overflow into all that is fluid en fluxus flooding in vertiginous vortices spiralling in intersticial surfaces re-produced as a pliant supplies re-(ap)plied in this supple place spliced per space splayed out in "a quantity of connection" that claim me [noun and name me]

in indeterminate endurance as meme memes me in mimesis when i am [meme myself 'nthememe] when i am [only a memes to an end] And i can't sememe in myself because i am simulacric. a memetic mutation. (in the memetime)

meme i me my maybe

So, even if i **seem** same it's only "effects" of the same. Like, you are not identical but eidedical. Deictical. A profusion of differences, appearances that play in a **locality** (which is) **an interlocuted linkage**. When locus allocated in likeness

i am always virtual. "a la mode" in the mode of. modelled on a modicum. **in the manner of** (mod.). en vogue. [vaga] vague — i'm inexact. A textatic act — **potent**ially metaphorical — **As if.** As if i was s(if)ting through these letters. **As if** you could hear me now. As if i **was** i. **As if** i could posess my own thought. Process my []. **As if** it was mine. as this moment p(r)oses for you. As i write the local, immediate, concrete re-created in my{t[h([i]{s)tory}] (yr [i]'s now) thres**hold** me. When i am **never** i / am always **as** you. Like it. Naked before you. in a struggle of silences on silence in disappearance when beyond the veil or under the veil is to look at the veil revile when the truth shall make you veiled "veil [as if] / the veil" of unknowing. valency veils. when everything **is** veil (veil smear) valor or an unveiling **unavailable** veiling [it avails/ not] violating in evol volumes.

Phonetically transliterated, between the two Mems should be a "Yud" [׳]. Kabbalistically read, the "yud" occupies the place of displacement, the space of the "excluded middle." Graphematically resembling a comma or apostrophe it signifies an absent present. As in the mark of the "pataphysical (the superinducement of the superinducement), the "Yud" references the elision of the elision which becomes quotation. So, as the doubled mark of an open quotation, it self-reflexively legitimizes and delegitimizes, simultaneously framing, fetishizing each Mem — (closing the closed Mem and opening the open Mem).

Ethnographically, the "Yud," as *Yuden* as Jude stands in for the Jewish people — a linguistic community constructed in and through language — constructed and defined [framed] by Torah (the revealed and concealed, the accessible and inaccessible).

Further, the "Yud" exists as the first letter of the Tetragrammaton. Therefore, as the orthographic mark of metaphoric elision ("patareferentially absenting presence and presenting absence) the "Yud" questions the possessed possessed through an unanswerable process of "imaginary solutions," a di/efferential process of supplement and desire.

The suffix functions as a pluralizing gesture, referencing multiplicity, excess. It foregrounds a space where the signified becomes a signifier — an ever-shifting supplemental process. For, in arguing for sameness, it masks difference and instead of the definable object, Mem (*la même chose*), it produces a chain of differential relations foregrounding language as a system of hyperreferential signs.

Through an interlingual process of redoubling the simple, the syntagm engages in a complex praxis of linking reference to structure (where form performs itself through content and content is reformed as a forum of frames), enacting the process of revealing and concealing, discovering and recovering as an ongoing semi(o)tic activity.

Beginning and ending with a Mem, orally the syntagm exists as a virtual palindrome and therefore deconstructs notions of origin and closure. By embodying difference within sameness it foregrounds repetition as a reproductive process.

Read backwards or forewards, it re-interprets itself in an (in)finite process of self-replicating metastability through a virally multiplicitous linguistic praxis — or misread as *mayim*: [water and Torah (Hebrew)], Mem amasses [links] a grammatological topocentrism to a fluid process of heterogenous excess, yet cross linguistically and self-reflexively signifies a hermeneutic process through its name.

in persecutory circuitry

sacrificed as

this trace /
effaces

FACE IT

as you fuse **into**
reph(r)ased in my face / frays
fission for / diffused or
INFESTED, faster i

face off

a resettled
recit re/cited as
reset cedes

            swerves

So, **slay** me down
'n over

ScRIPt out of

       anthropophagis
       these pages
       eidetic, paripatetic
       pa(thetic

     pata / scitical
      exitical

          **[when the succubus is
            calling us]**

when **TH'IS IS THE DESTROYED**

Decimated.
Asunder.

thrashed in the sweat of

i comma, comma, comma
home to —
　　this homocidical deictic

when **this** home, homeosis
a homily — a
rotting homologue —

A homeopat(h)alogical lacuna

grinds

　　this myth

　　　　(as my \
　　　mouth
　　slips)

Miming,

　　　　　　　　not me — **MY[T(HI{STORY, baby** —

in this moratoria topoi
this patamorphic rasp

shattered

diffused
in **that** mirror, the error
i made —

notating
t'ain / per tain
twined contaminated or
quanti-tainted in
this 'patacidical

maintenance
this main tennance
maintained / detained

in **spontenaity**
tainted in

a profusion of presence
this promise or
premise this

possibility poised

as tensor sends
in resinous ends

when to name is to remember
                dismember
                december

AS IF s(if)ting

    in desire / and
    disappearance

spared in
surface excises

ex-schize me

in this irreducible t'error
the horror of
this myth

    theodicy
    as this odyssey

i collapse
in you

like / as kin
as skin / and i'm askin'
seekin' this kin

as i take you up

**[in
and / for
love]**

in this rigorous drift
riven with

this viscera
invested in

[the risk of difference]

the sum of
semas semes
when the same is

as distrust swells
ceremoniously

sucked in the
steaming slash

when to give
is to contaminate

                           poisoned

in possibility
as the bliss
of the abyss
bears abymming

A ban(donned in

                                         degenerescence,
                                            dehiscences
                                               abcesses

when you t'ache me in the
blur of

when you are taken for
get taken up or / in
fact, taken as
a given.

g[if]ts

give it away
give it away
give it away, now

as i give over to
or am gifted by in
fragments —

for what i got /
gotta give it up / gonna get it /
Gotta give it

to you

p'resented in the
s'leurre of

how to give
to take to
give to

as you steal into
this appropriative apparati
errati

                    ciphered as
                an interscepted surplus
                    supplements

this grift graven as
es gibt. given

for what' due,

            (fort-da des dü)

caressed as
the rest excessed
as portent tains
retains [retiens]

        tearing at

this **infected** flex
as skein suckin'

savouring
not mystery
but my history

my(t[history
my hystereses —

as silences slip /

      lisp splits

jouir (en)je(u)-i-sense

je suis
ensouciance

je-i-sans(e)
issuance
jew ess

     sans

         errance.

in the appearance of i

arise and go now [agon]
abcesses on the H'i

rhyzome

re-leases
seizes
de ceases zones of

hystereses. restorying

these ecstasies

**KEEPS ON REISEN
REISEN**

in metalepsis as

ellipse slips
abcesses

So, cut me some s/lack

As you get glossed, lost
inside

                    this simulacric axis

                       EXUSE ME:
                      EXCURSE ME:

                                   (in this)

excisive elision
residual derision
d'elusive vised
in yr i's

this ragin' errative
regenerative
reaching for —
re-charged or

So, say hey babe,

TAKE A WALK ON THE WILD SLIDE

pseuded in these ties

UNTIE MEME
UNTIME ME

in ptomain(s) tain
demain
de**means this**. you sd
domain —

   tenets —

contaminated in
A patac(r)itical sucking
a synechdoche diectic

dis [sic] ecrit
dis-eased

Not protocal
but a patacall

                    beyond and beside calling

as mekabel, kabal
cables or
calls on

Because my call,

                    A close call

                DO YOU WANNA CALL IN —

in Hebraic breakage

(bracketing

THIS BARAGE

when you reek of
this wreckage —

                    rapt in

absorbed in / these orbits
an exacerbated about

beaten out of

this bliss —
as accessory seeps
in impasse
a pata pass

abstracted

when my call's
a cruising caress —

you are a player

a pliant
appelez placed

A hyperspace

sapping

in this ensouciant insistence
resistent

You are a sapir

sucking me out
through yr
pata scitation

cradled in the curve of

vague intent wavering ridges drift legitimated in a raging hunger
mounted in the spread darkness of

your face temples eyes

as i rages in adjacency, in appearance in remora. a memory. a
liminal anomaly as distances stream. mounted in tension cells /
swelling insistent displaced in exclusion / compounding in

the trace of an ending yet [] never closing sign of [your] name

in a resistent insistence
resurgent censors subordinated i/nexus

        in circuitous sediment

wanting

        what's outside of these sides
        when apside sites are
        re/scited

        when i am beside myself

matted in reckless
exile   enmeshed inside and beneath wanting

the spur of

    aporitic power which
    appears **AS** power
    pro**priot**ous / as
    p(our) **FOR** power
    performs

                writ(h)ing in ganglia root moss
                ammassed

as i steal away

    in desire
    incendiary diario
    enscenderia dare i / o —
    s'end'err or
    this danger

poisoned on the edge of
when you are already gone

and i am

absorbed in a body
impress framed by

this memory
swells

in immediacy / in madness. in fear and aroused in the rasp of yr
voice entangled in an interdiscursive
resurgence. diffused in

when i am   marked by / the anonymous

horror of
yr absence

displaced in surplus spreads

I have shared your shadow
screams / and before mourning

whose permanence is

also that —

i inhabit you
elsewhere

when i emerge **from** you

as i collapse in
the pleasure of
the scar is
the trace is the memory

// reconstructed . when the wound is
a shared frontier

what is mine when i am

fused in
resonance in nearness as
surrender swells

scarred in the gashes of coagulent traces

So, i can't sememe in myself because i am constructed
in the face of —

[but i feel so real]

C'mon get real —

Really, it's producing only effects of the real.

It's all play. Appelez. As i put it into [] as i
come out and [] in a
field of interplays.
Just common plays — plies plais or placates
as i call **into** and
re-play

this homage an image

(hyperreal and inauthentic)

A memetic mutation
made en mode modelled on

What is mine —

And what do i want in wanting in the fragments of yr face
re-phrased in face value. [Aphasic] to save face. In
phase facing /

(which is an about face)   facilitated in virtual turns or

a reproduction of profiles —

your face.

      contorted by tics and
        bathed in an anxiety

When you have gone mad

        in the [at](tic)
        (or in the act of)

              substitution. transfers.

        syntactic racks
      the auratic (n)e(u)rotic
      erratic wrought with

WHAT IS A TIC —

a battle between the face
that tries to escape
the face and the face itself Dismantling
the face. A gesture effaced in
Lies. between. the face. As the syntax
enacts. "[] an index" articulates. The face
a fa(r)ce. A fable. As yr face lifts fastened to / or faster
you face up to / and fascinate

      Meme my face and i

in swamp mottled sedges wrought / in a sequence of bason basks
or flax fielded

in proximity / and i am carried
in all yr **mor**phology

emerge **into** a presupposition or precipice position. held by
what's **propre** an
appeal or price of an appropriative process as a premise, a
promise, pro-mises
i am tied **to** you — propelled by impropriety — dictated or
dedicated / in a dialectic of
decisions

in the dead scent of

focused / not without
fear / without debt /
without voice abject. / Among

tracery echoes of coarse moss yellow scummed slough in the
dead scent of rusted fragments when

T'erritory is an act of rhythm

Terrified, i only wanted to touch you —

excised as

all [i's] as

l'objet delies —

in irreducible slides /
elides

      i cd die
      i cd love you
      i cd —

when this fiction reels

in friction —
or fractions of fact
infects fiction as
a complex flex of
conflictual flax
for facts in flux
is alway infact
fiction

in appearance and
promise in

apotropaic ochre
or an echoic ecrit

secretes —

as a cathexis
i'nexus annexes
in excess
'n axis of

adjacency

Because i cannot locate you

                                        dislocated
                                        locuted

clots as scum swells
in the stench of

syntactic
(n)e(u)rotics. rotting
wrought in

striated constraint —

                        Absence
                        of stained /

                                surfaces
                                Abcessed

"In excess, that is where I become you, and excess never belongs to itself"

[Irigaray]

(in the echo of embrace

as i pass **between**

"this possibility
   of place"

consequently, collective
and becoming

surface(s) as historicies lapsus as
centers surge swimming in
the midst of aural memory a glasseous
maximus (up so floating) tremulous
in these words a
porous process

   placed in a sonorous sensorium

ungrounded i
move. on /

as history passes through

as i write you out of
as you appear
appropriating this place

[putting me in my []

//up-rooted in
and without grounds

as i lay on the moist earth

((foregrounding))) // hard against me

gathers
thresholds. as i (edge into —

To get a hold on

this place displaced in
a field of interplays in a system of
palimpsestic re-placings where
each place matted in
a "universe of discourse"

a plaisure.

because there **is no** place to go back to —
when there's always receiving
an extravag(r)ance of

in an untouched surface of meaning whose every gesture is reflexive
/ whose every gesture an effect
of capturing a surface that becomes more
enclosed the more it expands

in the length of
an extatic masastacy

an exilic past. "ex-sists" in excess or exceeds as "ex cedere" (to
pass beyond, out of; ex-cidere falls outside of; disposessed from;
ex-cidere to detatch by cutting, excised i am cut off and **into**
slysdexic doxa

etc.

Because being Jewish means exiling
yourself in the word and at the same
time weeping for your exile [Jabés]

in a tainted reign. a night train or textual strain

[conjunction junction what's yr function]

as logomachia makes
méconnaises
kinesis in
ne me qui te critiques

So, c'mon baby do the logomotion with me

sacrificed
in sundrawn sweat and sweetgrass

in this lost lacuna where

                              everything otiumic
                              everything blue

                              sky / sea

apostrophic
and spoken for

          when absence
          as silence is
          scarless

scattered
as risk and scoria

in echolocation clicks
(a)quiesced

As murmers merge at the margins of
what happens in the margins is what
happens

hovered in

a history of images a mirage. merges. as mere murmers. sus-
tained in names. nomos. nomy by no means anonyma. nemo
anima nom anon numina dehiscences. abcesses. climbing toward
absence through fretwork and fractures — so no

"today [i] shall not find [you] in the field" (Beschalach)
— so far afield, or by field he sd. it ws a "savage
field" (Lee) a "field of conflict" (Davey), a "Field
[of] Notes" (Kroetsch), a "field of struggle" (Foucault)

slashed in
moist black fields
about the slough

unsettled

in a syntactic nomadics
in rank weeds
sun-dogs and stars

['cuz i'm unforghet(to)able]

a tracery of scars
curves as
synechdochic spreads
spared by

what i omitted
what i wanted to forget

what i forgot to remember:

(in 200 K by 11)
7, 93, 14, 90, 144 thresholds

this history of
admission

FÖRBJUDEN

48, 35, 121 North
Coboconk, Minden
this stretch of highway
as old ingoldsby inn ends

Lake Simcoe
Lake Lochlin
Kashagawigamog rock face

forested in cedar shields
shouldered by
and should i /

      wield shards
      i share you

as solyps spill
in satiate shades —

      striated in

this pseudonymous signing

08, 13, 93, 80 K's out of
up county corners
where the train
grounded in woodlots:

        seeders and binders
      harrow in the reap wrought
      threshing
      in the summer fallow

        granary

and
tribe
specific

Hebrew / Habiru: It remains unclear
whether the term was meant as an
adjective to describe widespread
groups of wanderers, adventurers
brigands detatched from city and
or as a noun to designate a
people

"when the word is bound to the word" I am names, words, horses, manes. As the word shatters the word suspended Words, sundrugged horses, manes, words. "Horses; who will do it? out of manes, words will do it, out of manes" "word[s], galloping, [mane[s] swollen with storms." sweating white horses manes. wet sweat horses **names**: when i've screamed myself hoarse. names what the horror say: "dehors" names abhors "ponees / of sweet disordr"

"I have compared thee, O my love, / to a company of horses"

hors texte? no hors-jeu

endlessly errant and
out of bounds

when i am not mad
but nomadic

when "The Jew inherited the Name and at
the same time lost h[er] place on
earth. The nomad takes on h[er]self
the unstated Name" [Jabés]

as borders deborder in aborderblur
deported

when i am
hinged to
this pleasure which is never this moment

when i am always running to find you
wedged in walls.
borders. laws.

**when madness is law
and law is madness**

So, when the sojourner is always a stranger
{etran-je[w]}
sans.

swells
in intransigent surges

        as j'ouis sens
        (jeu)ne naissance
        as jouissance
        i-nnascence

spirals. en pillars. compars. vortices

as systems in context surfaces as a surplus censors
in proximity i'nexus

as plexus extends
in turrets and trellis / russett
matrices of removal

when

        "[the] Jews [] have a vested interest solely in
        de(con)struction and never order"

        [Hitler, "War Speech, 1945"]

"To be sent away from your city was to be deprived of communal protection and to be made an outcast, a Habiru"

bursting in violence and enflamed memory

once upon
i came to you

when i could not
be integrated, converted
or expelled

plied or played

when i came

as a territorial assemblage
lodged in

a "voKABALLAry"

when i came

as a choreography of
hysterical letters a
"chor-a" graphé excised
in a rustle of root
houses recesses
re-cited in
a r(elational spacing espaced en
an irrepressible presence /
as the w(a)nder of
appearance / expresences

Aibling Bad Alexandersbad Bad Antogast Bad Bbergzabern Bad Bellingen Ba
erka Bad Berneck Bad Bertrich Bad Bevenson Bad Bibra Bad Blankenburg Ba
ll Bad Bramstedt Bad Breisis Bad Bruckenau Bad Buchau Bad Camberg Ba
Bad Ditzenbach Bad Doberan Bad Dreiburgen Bad Driburg Ba
Bad Durrenberg Bad Durrheim Bad Eilsen Bad Elster Bad Elms Ba
Bad Feilnbach Bad Frankenhausen Bad Freienwalde Bad Friedrichshall Ba
Bad Grandersheim Bad Gogging Bad Gottleuba Bad Grund Bad Harzburg Ba
ermannsborn Bad Herrenalb Bad Hersfeld Bad Hohenstadt Bad Homburg Ba
angen Bad Iburg Bad Ionau Bad this bad's for you. Bad Ko en Ba
eimr Bad Klosterlausnitz Bad Kohlgrubeuern Bad Konig Bad hofen Ba
z Bad Kr gen Bad Laer Bad Lansensalza Bad Lauchstad Lausick Ba
Liebens Bad Liebenwerda Bad Liebezell Bad Lippspring Marienberg
ad Mar entheim Bad Munder Bad Munster Ebern g Ba tereifel Ba
eusta Bi Niedernau Bad Nuendorf Bad Ob stdorf it o bad. Ba
Bad etersta bad Pyrmount Bad Rappenau B Reichein Rippoldsau
ad R chehen Bad Saarow Pieskow this ud s for you achsa Ba
lzel irth B Salzhausen Bad Salzschli Bad Salzufle ngen Ba
mie berg ad Schussenried Bad Schvalbach Bad Schw Segemerg
ode llendrf ad Soden i feel so ba Salmu ster Bad Bad Sulz
ben d Tesnach avelstein Bad ennsta t Bad Tolz B gen Ba
B Wal iesborn Bad Waldsee Bad We ernkotte essee Ba
ilsn k Ba W mpfen Bad Windsha Bad orishofen zach Ba
bern Bad eckenstedt Badelshaus aden Bade enweile
 orn this bad's for you Bad Bberg heim Ba
Bernch Bad Bevenson Bad ibr enba
Breisis Bad Bruckenau Bad this Bad er and
Ditzenbach Bad Doberan Bad Dr

Durrenberg Bad Durrheim Bad Eilsen Bad Elster Bad Elms Bad Endbach Ba
nbach Bad Frankenhausen Bad Freienwalde Bad Friedrichshall Bad Fussing is s
rsheim Bad Gogging Bad Gottleuba Bad Grund Bad Harzburg Bad Heilbrunn Ba
Bad Herrenalb Bad Hersfeld Bad Hohenstadt Bad Homburg Bad Honnet Ba
l Iburg B   Karlshafen Bad Kissingen Ba
losterla   Konigshofen Bad Kosen Ba
rosi   d Lausick Bad Lauterber
n   arienberg Bad Meinber
eim   ffel Bad Nauheim Ba
Niedern   ad. Bad Oldesloe Bad Or
Bad Pyrmo   Rippoldsau Bad Rotenfels Ba
d Saarow Pieskow this bud's for you. Bad Sachsa Bad Sackingen Bad Salzdetturt
n Bad Salzschlirf Bad Salzuflen Bad Salzungen Bad Schandau Bad Schmiedeber
ried Bad Schwalbach Bad Schwartau Bad Segemerg Bad Soden Bad Sode
Soden i feel so bad Salmunster Bad Suderode Bad Sulza Bad Sulze Bad teben Ba
lstein Bad Tennstedt Bad Tolz Bad Uberkingen Bad Urach Bad Vilbel Ba
Bad Waldsee Bad Westernkotten Bad Wiessee Bad Wildungen Bad Wilsnack Ba
l Windsheim Bad Worishofen Bad Wurzach Bad Zwischenahn Badberge
lt Badelshausen Badem Baden Baden Badenweiler Badersleben Badschonborn Ba

"...the satanic and evil principle is embodied in the Jews, because they -- being a people without living space for two thousand years -- threaten to destroy the purpose of history". [Hitler]

for Michael

Published with the assistance of the Canada Council

Talonbooks
#201 - 1019 East Cordova
Vancouver, British Columbia
Canada V6A 1M8

Typeset in Palatino by Pièce de Résistance Ltée., and printed and bound in Canada by Hignell Printing Ltd.

First Printing: February 1994

ACKNOWLEDGMENTS: Earlier versions of "Feminine "Secreture" appeared as "Contextatic Sophistry" presented at Gesellschaft für Kanada Studien Conference, "Gender Differences and Institutions in Canada" in Grainau, & as "Sophistical Dismemberment" presented at the British Association for the Canadian Studies Conference, "Difference and Community: Canada and Europe," 1992 (Leeds). It was re-presented as a Lecture for Canadian Literature, at York University (Toronto), April, 1993, & as part of a Canadian Literature Field Exam, May, 1993. "Feminine "Secreture" was translated for performance as "A Canadian Feminist Poetics" for the Centre for Canadian Studies, Universidad de la Laguna (Tenerife, Spain) in December, 1993, & was later re-worked for the Institute of Commonwealth and American Studies and English Language Conference, "Commonwealth and American Women's Discourse," January, 1994 (Mysore, India). Selected portions were further re-formed as "The Empress Strikes Back," presented at the SNDT Women's University (Bombay) January, 1994. "Rigor Mo(r)ts: Death of Objectivity" was presented at the "Deadlines Conference" at SUNY (Buffalo) March, 1993. "N[or]th of Ar(c)ticulation" was first presented at the EGSA Colloquium, at York University, March, 1993; was reworked for the Workshop on Canadian Studies at the M. S. University of Baroda (Vadodara), January 1994; extended for performance at the University of Goa, January 1994; & is forthcoming in "The Foremost Investigations Anthology," Colorado, 1994. A previous version was published in *A Poetics of Criticism* (Buffalo, 1994). Earlier versions of "POETIX" were presented at the "Poetics Conference," SUNYAB, March, 1993, & appeared in *Writing from the New Coast Anthology* (December, 1993). Further selections of *Mêmewars* have appeared in *SinOverTan, Cabaret Vert, The Poetry Project, Oblek, TXT* & *Poetic Briefs*. THANKS TO: External Affairs and International Trade Canada, Much Music, Radio York, CIUT Radio, Cable 10 TV, CKY TV, Winnipeg TV, City TV, Co-Op Radio & the Knowledge Network. Also to Warren Tallman, bill bissett, Rabbi R. Cahana, Ken & Evan Karasick, Terry Goldie, Darren Wershler-Henry, Virus 23, Raymond Federman, Charles Bernstein, Shelley Spevakow & Kedrick James.

Canadian Cataloguing in Publication Data

Karasick, Adeena, 1965-
Mêmewars

Poems.
ISBN 0-88922-344-0

I. Title.
PS8571.A74M4 1993   C811'.54   C94-910007-2
PR9199.3.K37M4 1993

MêMewars

Adeena Karasick

Talonbooks Vancouver 1994